Sufism

A Bridge Between Religions

Professor Nader Angha
Pir Oveyssi

MTO
PUBLICATIONS ®

Nader Angha

Sufism: A Bridge Between Religions

ISBN 978-190491662-8

A catalogue record for this book is available from the British Library.
Published in Great Britain in 2011 by MTO Publications ®.
Printed in China by R.R.Donnelley

www.mto.org

Other Books by the same Author:

Peace
Sufism & Faith
Sufism: The Reality of Religion
Whispering Moments: Inspirations
Revelation (Elhām)
The Fragrance of Sufism
Theory "I"-The Inner Dimension Of Leadership
The Secret Word
Expansion & Contraction Within Being (Dahm)
Kanz-al-Soluk va Raaz-Nameh
The Approaching Promise
Masnavi Ravayeh
Sufism Lecture Series:
- Sufism
- Sufism and Peace
- Sufism and Knowledge
- Sufism and Islam
- Sufism and Wisdom

Contents

Introduction	Peter Schütt	VII
Chapter I	The Origin of Religion	1
Chapter II	What is Religion?	17
Chapter III	The "Being", the "I"	23
Chapter IV	Sufism	27
Chapter V	Freedom	35
Chapter VI	Unification	41
Chapter VII	What is "Muslim?"	49
Chapter VIII	The Bridge	53
Notes		59
Genealogy of Maktab Tarighat Oveyssi Shamaghasoudi (M.T.O.)-School of Islamic Sufism®		63

Introduction

The lecture, "Mysticism as a Bridge Between Religions", given by the Pir of the Oveyssi School of Sufism on February 17, 2000 in the historic building of the Hamburg "Patriotic Society of 1765" was a high point in the more than two hundred year history of this oldest German People's Initiative. The event, attended by approximately 1,000 guests from Hamburg and surrounding areas, near and far, was one of the quarterly meetings of "Inter-religious Dialogues", which has met since 1993 in order to find ways of improving communication between Christians, Jews, Muslims, Buddhists and Hindus.

The "Patriotic Society" was an ideal host for the Pir of the Oveyssi School, for the concept of tolerance is already deeply anchored in its founding documents. The society was founded according to the British model of the times, when Gotthold Ephraim Lessing, the author of Nathan der Weise (Nathan the Wise), was working as a dramatic adviser in the Hamburg National Theater and was engaged in a bitter feud with the custodians of Lutheran orthodoxy. The "Patriots" of Hamburg stood up, in the beginning for very mercantile motives, for the legal emancipation of non-Lutheran minorities in the Hanseatic town, for the Jews who had immigrated from Spain and Portugal, for the Persian merchants in the free port, for the Catholics and for the Mennonites, Quakers, and other Protestant minorities persecuted in Holland and England. They established communication between the various religious beliefs and thus not only contributed to inner peace, but also to the economic rise of the "Free and Hanseatic Hamburg", which considered itself a "Gateway to the World"— thus reads the heraldic motto — and which as an oceanic commercial center was dependent on good relationships with people all over the world.

Today, religious life in Hamburg is more diverse than in any other major German city. The religious atlas of Hamburg includes 98 different religious communities and congregations, which are associated with all the great world religions. Less than half of Hamburg's inhabitants are Christian. The Jewish congregation again has more than 1,000 members. The Buddhists have about 15,000 individuals in their various centers. The number of Muslims has risen to over 120,000. Many of them belong to the Schura (Islamic Assembly), which has 44 Islamic organizations associated with it. For a teacher of Islamic Mysticism such as Hazrat Pir, who is open toward contact with followers of other religions, the Hanseatic town is an ideal sounding-board. This is the third guest lecture for Hazrat Pir in Hamburg in the past decade. His first lecture took place at the Eastern Studies Department of the University of Hamburg and his second lecture took place at the Institute of Eastern Studies. He was invited by Professor Dr. Udo Steinbach, who has since written an introduction to Hazrat Pir's book entitled Sufism, the Reality of Religion.

Anyone who has read the writings of the Master of the Oveyssi School, or has been able to experience one of his lectures and observe how he develops his ideas, will confirm that the Oveyssi Pir is one of the most impressive and influential religious figures of this epoch. Even someone who encounters him with doubt cannot evade his spiritual charisma. Without his dynamic character, energy, and creative nature, the phenomenal expansion of Oveyssi School over half the world within one generation would not be explainable, for the network now reaches from Australia over Europe to North America and includes half a million followers. His students all over the globe exemplify a non-violent, gentle, free and open-minded Islam. In his school there is, as the Quran instructs, no compulsion in faith, and he does not ask anyone to change their religion to Islam. He teaches neither with a sword nor with proclamations; his arms are clear words, good examples, and ethically exemplary deeds. His aim is the re-spiritualization of our lives, not only of ourselves, but also of our family and society.

Hazrat Pir would like to contribute to social health by helping to better our relationship with our creator and protector, God, and also with our fellow creatures and human beings. This healing power is felt by almost everyone who enters an Oveyssi Khaneghah. Friendly, happy, energetic, confident and healthy, in the best sense, these people make a lasting impression on the soul and society everywhere.

The period of spiritual awakening and renewal introduced by the Oveyssi Pir does not stand alone, but is part of a world-embracing renaissance of the religions. The agnostic German philosopher Jürgen Habermas recently remarked, with a roguish undertone, "The good old God, whom we believed to have been put ad acta long ago, has made his way back into human history in a both impressive and cunning manner." From the Falun-Gong movement in China to the rediscovery of the Buddhist heritage in Southeast Asia, from the reincarnation of Hindu celebrations and rituals on the Indian subcontinent to retrospective reflection on Christian liberation theology in Latin America, from the formation of new esoteric trends in Western countries to the re-strengthening of Sufism and brotherhood in many Muslim countries, the signs accumulate worldwide that humans have again begun to focus on their religious roots after the complete failure of atheistic ideologies in the 20th century. It goes without saying that in such periods of upheaval some false prophets would also like to take advantage of the favorable moment and try to dupe people. This makes it even more necessary in questions of belief to speak a clear language and to separate the truth from the lies.

The language of the Oveyssi Pir, in spite of poetic and metaphoric language, leaves nothing to be questioned as far as clarity is concerned. It is, in spite of complete solidarity with the 1400 year old tradition of his school, highly modern, yet not presumptuously so. It is mystically inspired, yet at the same time scientifically exact. He speaks of the mystical way of enlightenment with the reliability of a modern natural scientist. He brings religion and philosophy, inspiration and research, physics and metaphysics into unity.

The voice of the Oveyssi Pir is increasingly heard. His word is asked for and needed—especially after the terrible news of September 11, 2001. Even though Hazrat Pir did not predict the course of events one and a half years before the terrorist attacks on the World Trade Center in New York, one still finds in his inspired and inspiring lecture several hints as to how a person penetrated by the spirit of Sufism could keep a clear head and trust in God even in the face of such catastrophes. One will search in vain for political instructions for action from him, yet will find even more inspiration and suggestions as to how each one of us can find self-enlightenment, come to terms with himself and his God, and therefore regain inner peace, which is the mental and spiritual prerequisite for the overcoming of hate, war, and injustice in the world.

Peter Schütt:

Peter Schütt is the spokesman for "Inter-religious Dialogues" and has also made a name for himself as a narrator. His latest publications are the short story collections *Emergency Landing in Turkmenistan: Three Quarter Hundred Short and Small Stories* and *Allah's Sun Laughs over Alster: 111 Stories from the 1002 Nights.*

In the name of God,
Most Gracious, Most Merciful

Chapter I
The Origin of Religion

What is religion? How did religion start? These questions have baffled philosophers, religious scholars, social psychologists and other academics for centuries. Scholars in such disciplines have pondered the answers to these questions, and have written numerous, yet often contradictory books on the above questions. Various disciplines often attempt to define religion as if it were somehow their exclusive property, using concepts, terms and vocabulary of the particular field, rather than adopting a multi-disciplinary perspective. Let's briefly examine the kinds of perspectives they have presented.

A modern dictionary[1] gives the first, or preferred, definition of religion as: "Concern over what exists beyond the visible world, differentiated from philosophy in that it operates through faith or intuition rather than reason, and generally including the idea of the existence of a single being, a group of beings, an eternal principle, or a transcendent spiritual entity that has created the world, that governs it, that controls its destinies, or that intervenes occasionally in the natural course of its history, as well as the idea that ritual, prayer, spiritual exercises, certain principles of everyday conduct, etc., are expedient, due, or spiritually rewarding, or arise naturally out of an inner need as a human response to the belief in such a being, principle, etc.".

Countless philosophers in diverse times and places throughout history have offered divergent and contradictory definitions and explanations of religion, from the early Greeks, through Hegel, Mill ("the essence of religion is the strong and earnest direction of the emotions and desires toward an ideal object, recognized as of the highest excellence and as rightfully paramount over all selfish objects of desire."[2]) and Marx, (religion...is the opium of the people), down to the present day. Huxley, using the term Philosophia perennis coined by Leibnitz, describes religion as *The Perennial Philosophy.*[3]

Anthropologists[4] have attempted to describe the religious practices of various groups, especially those they considered more "primitive", hoping to discover the nature of religion by examining its beginnings.[5] They have also attempted to determine whether or not all human groups possess some form of religion. So far they have been unable to find one that clearly does not.

Sociologists have often seen religion as a social product, based on social needs and serving societal purposes. In other words, they see religion as man-made, created in order to meet social goals. In this case, the deity is seen as a creation of mankind.

Psychiatrists and psychologists either avoid, implying its unimportance and lack of relevance in human behavior, or ultimately are forced to consider religion, resulting in diametrically opposed points of view. Freud's ideas are perhaps best known: he considered religion to be a "universal obsessional neurosis of humanity", and stated: "religion is an illusion and it derives its strength from the fact that it falls in with our instinctual desires."[6] He also considered it a danger to individual development.

In marked contrast, Jung valued religion, and saw the true religious experience, which he considered to be internal, numinous, and personal, as separate from religious institutions, which he criticized.[7] Later psychologists have differentiated between esoteric and exoteric or intrinsic versus. extrinsic religiosity, noting that the two types are almost opposites of one another.[8] The externally focused orientation, sometimes called immature religion, provides status and security. The internally focused is considered mature, integrated and an end in itself.

A fable from Lincoln Steffans affirms Jung's point of view. "A man climbed to the top of the highest mountain, and there, standing on tiptoe, seized hold of the truth. Satan, who had suspected mischief from this upstart, had directed one of his underlings to follow him. When the demon reported with alarm the man's success—that he had seized hold of truth—Satan was unperturbed. "Don't worry" he yawned. "I'll tempt him to institutionalize it."[9]

Mythologists try to claim religion as their own, diminishing it to the mold of merely another form of story guiding human behavior. For example, Joseph Campbell's well-known four volume descriptive series on various past and present mythologies of the world is titled *The Masks of God.*[10]

Modern "hard" scientists are now observing parallels between such seemingly diverse areas as biochemistry, quantum physics and the religious experience. They are discerning that contemporary "science" is being forced to re-evaluate what religion has traditionally taught, in scientific terms.[11]

The truth is simple. In the beginning people were fearful of the powerful forces of nature and of all the natural phenomena. They feared the sun and the moon, earthquakes and thunderstorms, flood and drought. They feared each other—fearing animosity, conflict, hatred and war. They were filled with needs as well as personal desires and wishes. Observing such powerful events, people inevitably came to worship these forces, considering them manifestations of gods. As stated by Hume: "The first ideas of religion arose not from a contemplation of the works of nature, but from a concern with regard to the events of life, and from the incessant hopes and fears which actuate the human mind."[12]

Gradually, people, out of their senses and imagination,[13] began to construct representations of these powerful forces and they created images as symbols for them. People believe symbolizing things makes them easier to deal with. People like to create representations or symbols, for doing so seems to reduce anxiety. It appears to quell a need for control of the uncontrollable. With symbols, we can and do fool ourselves.

So in order to be able to quell their fears, protect themselves and satisfy all their needs and desires, people devised representations or symbols which signified the forces impinging on human life. When a representation, an image, is of a deity, something which is worshiped, we call it an idol. The first idols were symbols for the unknown forces which shape the physical universe and strongly impact human life and behavior. In other words, they stood for it, and fooled the susceptible mind into believing that they were accessible, and since they were accessible, they could now be controlled. They convinced themselves that through prayers, petition, perhaps sacrifice, or some other activity, one could be spared from the unpleasant events which marred the lives of others. They lost sight of the simple truth that symbols stand for something, but they are not the thing itself. A symbol can suggest some kind of identification, but a symbol is not reality.

An idol was something for which they could provide ceremonies, and people love ceremonies. Naturally they first created the idols, of wood, stone, and precious metals such as gold and silver, then a site for the idols and places of worship. They would take gifts and offerings to such places, hoping for their desires to come true or their problems to be solved, without realizing that all these symbols they had created were perishable, impermanent, changeable, the products of their own imaginations, and would not be able to provide the benefits they were looking for.

Out of fear, desire and hope, they created various symbols, various idols which became their gods, then they provided places in which to worship these deities. They made sacrifices and invented special rituals for gods like Mars and Jupiter, Venus and Neptune. As Aristotle noted, gods who were fashioned in the image of people. These practices continued for long years.

As politicians around the world well know, symbols can gradually gain the power or capacity to invoke strong emotional responses, particularly to susceptible people. The dictionary tells us that a symbol has "a complex of associated meanings and (is) perceived as having inherent value separable from that which is symbolized...."[14] Idols are symbols, not reality, but people mistook them for reality. Gradually, the symbols became more important than the reality, and began to be valued far beyond their minimal worth, coming to mean more than the actual reality.

We are all at least somewhat aware of the emotional power the representations or symbols may come to possess. A flag comes to symbolize our country, and we are stirred when we see it waving. We are aware, at least historically, that the cross has come to represent a particular religious tradition, and people of that tradition frequently wear the symbol. People will fight for, and even give their lives for such symbols.

So, for many centuries people had man-made objects shaped as their gods, which they had provided for themselves in their places of worship, just as they desired and hoped. People worshiped their own creations, their representations of reality.

However, eventually people came to tell the others that their representations, their way of worship, was incorrect. They stated that there is a way, a true path, which leads to reality and is preferable to what they were doing. These people were called Prophets. One of the earliest prophets was Abraham, described in the (Holy Qur'an 6:74-79):

> 74. Lo! Abraham said to his father Azar: "Take your idols for gods? For I see you and your people in

manifest error."

75. So also did We show Abraham the power and the laws of the heavens and the earth, that he might (with understanding) have certitude.

76. When the night covered him over, he saw a star. He said: "This is my Lord." But when it set, he said: "I love not those that set."

77. When he saw the moon rising in splendor, he said: "This is my Lord." But when the moon set, he said: "Unless my Lord guide me, I shall surely be among those who go astray."

78. When he saw the sun rising in splendor, he said: "This is my Lord; This is the greatest (of all)." But when the sun set, he said: "O my people! I am indeed free from your (guilt) of giving partners to Allah.

79. For me, I have set my face, firmly and truly, towards Him Who created the heavens and the earth, and never shall I give partners to Allah."

The prophets were sent by God, and they told the people that what they had created for themselves as gods had limitations and boundaries and were not stable, but obviously had a tendency to change, altering form and shape with every individual imagination and interpretation. The prophets said that God was all-powerful, omniscient, and supreme. Then the prophets told the people about how they could inquire into the reality of God, which was stable and unchangeable. They told of how far more benefits in everyday life and in social affairs would be attained. The prophets, such as Buddha, Jesus, Moses, and Mohammad (peace be upon them), spoke the truth. The prophets told the people: "We have been inspired by God; we are in unity with God." As Jesus said: "I and my father are one (John 10:30)."

Of course the people, after much debate about what the prophets were saying, finally accepted their statements, but just as words, not as truth. They did not accept the teaching in the way they should have, for they had accepted merely out of obedience, not because they knew God or had any communication with God. And they did not understand that the road to God was through self-experience and self-knowledge, through cognizing the reality of God. Instead they accepted the prophets' words only in relation to their own needs and desires, and their own perceptions. With such a lack of understanding, the old thoughts and ways easily returned. Moses had only to leave for 40 days for the people to construct a golden calf to worship (Holy Qur'an 2:51, 2:92).

People shaped the teachings of the prophets to their liking, to symbolic terms. Now in place of idols made of stone or wood, the idols were constructed of words, which are simply verbal symbols.[15] And as was preached in a 1686 sermon, “Words are the signs and symbols of things; and, as in accounts, cyphers and figures pass for real sums; so ...words and names pass for things themselves".[16] But they are not the things. And, as my father indicated; "Words cannot transfer the meaning".[17] The eloquent phrases and philosophical flights of fancy came to be the new objects of adoration.

So once again there were a multitude of idols in the places of worship. This time, people had once again used their reasoning and imagination to create new idols in their own minds, and in the houses of worship. They replaced their idols with the god which took shape through their imagination, which in their view had been introduced by the prophets. However, their understanding was far from the truth, for it was still based on their personal needs and desires.

We do the same today, symbolizing everything, including God. God is imagined as a white-haired, bearded and robed old man sitting in the clouds. This idol, this representation in their minds, was created and many people accepted it. The well-known anthropologists Durkheim, Radcliffe-Brown and Malinowski, familiar with other cultures, concluded that the symbols people use “...‘reflected’or ‘expressed’ social structure...”.[18] In other words, they believed social groups created religious symbols in their own image, including this symbolization of God with the physical characteristics of a human male.

We fail to remember that a symbol stands for something; it is not the thing itself. We come to behave as if the representation were the reality. The symbol may become more important, more potent than the reality it represents. As indicated in an earlier work:

> Now, if I were to come and tell you about God, and what I told you did not cross-reference with the image you have in your mind of God, you would either say, “He’s crazy”, or "He doesn’t know." Whereas, if the words that I spoke about God had formed an image in your mind early on, that would be the basis for the measurement of information. In either case, the information you have collected is invalid and void of knowledge. If you look closely, you will see that your understanding of God was based on what others had described to you, and not your own experience. You had merely accepted what others had said.[19]

Over decades and centuries, what the symbol is supposed to stand for may gradually change so that the original representation is gradually transformed into a different image which bears little resemblance to the original. Then the initial meaning of the symbol may become lost. Two modern examples are that of the devil, and of heaven. There is a widely accepted Western representation of the devil as a man with horns and a forked tail, dressed in red, carrying a pitchfork. This image is, of course, outside ourselves, sometimes pictured as whispering in our ears. This is a personification, a symbol which has become so powerful that few people today recognize that the reality of the "devil" is the cellular level of our own being. They do not understand that the "devil" is within us.

The same process has occurred with Heaven. It has come to be considered in physical terms as an actual place, as a beautiful garden, with flowers, fruits and flowing rivers, high above us in the clouds, with angels playing harps. Who today recognizes that this is only a symbol for the reality of Heaven, which is a state of being? Heaven is also within us, not without.

In both these cases, the emphasis on the symbol has become misleading, actually leading people away from the reality it represents. It is often easier to be satisfied with such a symbol than to accept a reality which would have powerful consequences for us. People become adapted to circumstances. We come to believe what we say even when we know it is not true.

All that people have actually done is to replace the different physical idols with their own mentality, their own desire for what profited them. Most people obviously have this tendency to believe in what they like or want rather than to believe what is really needed, and tend to do what suits them rather than what is possibly beneficial for them. Whatever we are most desirous of attaining, whatever we devote ourselves to, whatever we think about most often is what we really worship. For example, it is said people worship money, position, power or fame.

From the time of the prophets onward, the saints, philosophers and true thinkers of the world decided to explain and present the way of learning/cognizing which the prophets had taught over a period of time. Then gradually, because of varying presentations in different societies, divergent groups emerged, according to their own particular schools of thought, considering themselves different religions because of differences in specific types of rituals or words associated with worship services. Time passed, so along the way it was seventeen years, then seventeen hundred, and so on.

Through the centuries many battles have been fought, ostensibly over these religious differences in words and rituals, which seemed to have become more important than cognition of God. However, in reality the conflicts were over wealth or power, using religion as a mask for more ulterior motives. In the name of religion, from the beginning until the present moment, economic, political and governmental forces have created wars in the world in order to control or possess land, objects, income, and even people. Over the centuries, how many millions have died because leaders used religious symbols to emotionally fire them and religious terminology to mask their greed and voraciousness? And in how many parts of the world are people still dying today, ostensibly over religion, but actually to fulfill selfish ends?

The prophets taught us to love one another. We can see how well their teachings are being followed in the contemporary world, with vivid images of the consequences of stones, bullets, guns, and bombs. The practices of supposedly religious people are often in direct contradiction to the teachings of the prophets.

Often I ask students: If the prophets—Buddha, Moses, Jesus, and Mohammad (peace be upon them)—were in one room, would they fight? The answer is obvious, of course not. Sadly, many people are so jaded by the history of supposedly religious warfare that they have forgotten what the prophets really taught, and actually believe the prophets would fight with each other. They have forgotten the prophets were sent by God as guides to show us the way to Him.

In the past three to four hundred years, gradually, as the earth became smaller and boundaries were removed, people have been more easily able to travel. Immigrants from different countries have moved from one area to another, and presented their own culture and religious identity to their new neighbors wherever they arrived. So gradually the face of religion was changed due to the different ideas, cultures and behavior patterns, coming all the way down to recent times. Now they talk about "globalization", and we hear about "New Age" beliefs, and different people deciding to place their belief in chanting, magic, reincarnation, crystals, and so forth and so on. The ideas formed from the beginning about religion have persisted down to the present era of organized religions and pervaded the creation of new religions with economic and political foundations. These have not been able to answer their listeners properly nor relate to their individual aspects. Consequently, people have turned to new ideas, faddish perspectives, divergent groups. In summary, that is where religion came from.

Chapter II
What is Religion?

What, then, is religion? The practice of religion is often limited to individuals attending various religious institutions. The purpose of this practice varies, but includes fear of punishment, hope of reward for good deeds, feelings of guilt, soothing their soul, or for social and cultural purposes. But this is not the reality of religion.

In another book, *Sufism*, I have described the reality of religion:

> Religion is a discipline, a precise system of training, whereby each person is individually trained to discover a dimension within his or her own being where the divine attributes are manifested. It is the realization of attributes such as compassion, knowledge, selflessness, love, devotion, honor, trust and so on, attributes normally associated with saints of the past. This is the dimension of their being that the prophets discovered through their cognition of God that gave rise to their uniqueness, strength, and knowledge.[20]

A famous parable of Rumi's illustrates this point.[21] People were sitting around informally, chatting and discussing their ideas. Late into the night, a wise man among them invited them all into a large tent. It was a dark night, and in that tent it was even darker. The wise man positioned various people in different areas and asked them to explain what they were experiencing based on the object they were feeling. Each one touched a different part of the object that was in front of them. When they had finished they were asked to come out, and the wise man asked them to explain what it was that had been experienced through their physical senses.

Each one portrayed what he or she had understood through his or her feeling of touch. One described: "There was a post or column of some sort, which was holding something and was rough...". Another depicted a fan, which was rough and moving, changing the air within the tent. Another experienced a water pipe that was flexible and moving, and so forth. Each person had touched a different part of the object and perceived and described it based on the experience of his or her physical senses. Each disagreed with the others, based on his or her separate experience and own perception. An intense argument began.

One said, No, it was a post. It was holding something and it was this dimension, and so on ....

Another said, no, it was a fan.

The show went on, the argument went on, then the wise man removed the curtain and lighted the lamp (removed the veil of ignorance). The tent was opened, and the unknown object, which was an elephant, could be seen. The people who were fighting over their own presumptions about the object finally saw the reality of what existed.

Let me comment that I would frequently prefer to use that expression, "the veil of ignorance", but the term has been too often misused by the world and is habitually used in reference to different concepts. In reality, the veil of ignorance was removed and the reality was unveiled.

How had it felt for them? I always use this story as an example when I ask people: "How do you really know God exists?" They usually reply that their inward feeling assures them of the existence of God. But how much can one depend on so-called "feelings" and senses? If we depend on our senses to understand everyday life, we have a problem, because most things cannot be understood or grasped by the senses. We see, feel and hear in a very limited dimension. If attempting to understand our surroundings through the use of our senses easily leads to misunderstandings, then how can we trust our senses to discover something as vast and real as the universe, Existence, or what is called God? Even in science we depend on actual facts rather than just our perceptions and feelings;

science has carefully documented how our physical senses and perceptions repeatedly fool us.[22]

How can we depend on the social, cultural, and politically motivated descriptions which different societies have taught us or forced us to believe, one way or another, in the matters of definitions and behavior? Are societies absolute, or do they vary from place to place, from culture to culture, and from time to time?

How is it possible, using only one sense, to attain full satisfaction in any thought or action? Suppose you are lost in the desert, and are dying of thirst. Your throat is dry, your lips are parched, and you would give anything for water. If someone wrote the word "water" on a piece of paper and gave it to you, would it quench your thirst? Of course not. You need to drink the real thing. I already mentioned the example of using the sense of touch, feeling, and then making assumptions based on the imagination of the mind. This is like creating some sort of image of water in order to be able to soothe one's thirst.

How can I be able to hear the words and then be able to conceive the meaning? We already know that words do not contain the meaning. They are simply symbols for things. They are like a map, and a map is different from the territory it depicts. We can look at many maps of London, but can never know what London is like until we go there. How, then, can I be able to use my senses or imitate other people in order to reach the goals that they have set for me?

People imitate others, from birth onward. They follow without knowledge. They copy, doing just like what they see. Don't we argue that the misbehavior of children is based on what they see at home, on TV, in their society? We also say the mistakes and misfortunes of adults are founded on what they learned in childhood. Suppose we have a wise man, sitting and eating some fruit. The other person, who only imitates and follows, acts as if he is eating, but instead chews some hard object, not fruit. Obviously, he will end up having broken teeth. Then he will create this scenario in his mind and proclaim how dumb or crazy the wise man was.

Overall I am not denying the usefulness of the senses. They work quite well and can provide us the information to which they have access. But the question arises somewhere else, which I will explain later. Nevertheless, with the limitations of the senses, how can I be able to depend on the wording of the statements, the rules of other people in society, both before my time or thereafter, so that I can accept what they have said, which is convenient for me in my own life?

Look at how society has set up its definitions, and how people have respected the social renderings, acted upon and assumed them. Is it not possible that some things are not as limited as has been stated by society? This is true of just about everything. Let us consider an example. I asked a couple, husband and wife, a question people often ask in society, for which they have an explanation. “Are you faithful to one another?”

Automatically, because of society’s teaching, they all start thinking that perhaps one of them is doing something wrong in their community. Without such prejudice, suppose we ask the couple, “Are you faithful? Do you have trust? Do you depend upon and base everything in your life upon one another?” This does not imply what society has assumed, that someone has extra-marital activity in his or her life. Maybe we are talking about the foundation of unity. Perhaps we are talking about how they are supposed to be supportive of one another in every aspect of life. Maybe we are talking about how they are supposed to be encouraging each other toward the maximum goal of life. Thus we are not just searching for one aspect, i.e. what society is looking for and what society defines as what faith, trust and respect can and should be.

Chapter III
The "Being", the "I"

Consider this as another example. What can I, as an individual, depend upon to help me discover what "I", as a human being, am about? Am I supposed to accept whatever everyone else has said or will say? Would it be me? Am I supposed to accept the way other people see and feel things? Would I see and feel the same? Am I supposed to find everything of my being in other people? Would it describe me at all? Obviously not! But then, if that is the case, everything will remain unknown to me, a mystery. Everything is mysterious. What does one do?

The definition of the so-called human being is: a unique yet complex masterpiece. This does not mean that he has to follow every other person's thought. He does not have to follow anything that has been said. He does not have to depend solely on his senses. This is where the mystery comes from. Mysticism—everywhere I look and everything I look at is a mystery. What isn't? We use the word mysticism, which comes from ancient times. But everything is unknown, even though people infer only that as the unknown. What is not? Everything around me is unknown to me. If I really want to discover the unknowns, they are there, and I have to initiate their discovery. Other people do not have to define them for me.

So obviously, if I need to discover and define everything myself, I need a tool. This tool is knowledge. I have to be knowledgeable in just about everything. I have to know everything, then I will be able to deal with it properly. Knowing the word is knowing little. I have to discover what actually exists. Knowing is not in appearance, not in the definitions, not what has been written in other books, not in what society dictates to me. Don't make the mistake of thinking it is possible to acquire knowledge from just any institution. If I study and become a physician or a scientist or a philosopher or what have you, it is going to be fulfilling, but that is not what we are talking about when we say knowing. We are talking about absolute knowledge.

We do know the foundation of every science is mathematics, which provides information about the dimensions. We do know philosophy talks about behavior and appearances and the way in which individuals perceive things. We do know that science talks about changeable conditions, and so is still discussing appearances rather than the real aspect of the things. If I need to discover what the reality of a thing is, I have to have certain knowledge which goes beyond the limitations of the individual, of books, and even of nature.

Do not misunderstand me. I am not denying science. No indeed, for science has discovered many details useful for healthy and good lives for individuals. But science still has not discovered that inner being, the "I". We are able to talk about everything in society in terms of what does exist. But there is one aspect which has not been acknowledged or even discussed by the various aspects of religion, of science, or of society, which is the existence of the Self. That is the source of mysticism.

Chapter IV
Sufism

Mysticism means, or rather the correct word for it, is Sufism, and the word for Sufism is Erfan (Irfan). So what is Sufism? In the book *Sufism*, I have stated that:

> "Sufism is the essence of the prophets' teachings. It is the Way of the Prophets. It has existed since the beginning of human history, for its seed lies within every human heart. In each age, God has sent Prophets to lead the people to the knowledge of "Him", Zoroaster, Moses, Buddha, Jesus, David, Mohammad—to name a few. Each Prophet has given humanity unique instructions to be learned and mastered in order to progress on the inward journey toward "God". The great ninth century Sufi, Bayazid Bastami, described the history of Sufism by stating: "Its seeds were set at the time of Adam, they sprouted under Noah and flowered under Abraham. Grapes formed at the time of

> Moses, and they ripened at the time of Jesus. In the time of Mohammad, they were made into pure wine."[23]

Of course, peace be upon all of them. What is Erfan or Sufism? It is the path of knowledge—the path to this true Self. It is cognition of this entity in absolute form, with all its attributes and capabilities. This is the **reality of religion** and the essence of God's teaching, conveyed through the Prophets. This is Erfan or Sufism.

The Holy Prophet Mohammad (peace be upon him) has said in *Nahj-ol-Fesahe*:

> "Knowledge is not in the sky to descend upon you, nor is it in the earth to grow for you, but it is innate, hidden within you until the human being is recognized in his totality as an absolute being with all of his capabilities and capacities in every stage of his existence."

All efforts to discover and capture this hidden aspect of nature will be deemed insufficient and deficient. So when we talk about Sufism, we are talking about the reality of every individual, the reality beyond the limitations of the experiences of the senses, beyond accepting other people's behavior, beyond practicing false rituals, beyond blind mental belief. Each individual is subject to discovery of this inner being, this absolute knowledge within him or herself. The knowledge is there for him or her to attain. As the Prophet Mohammad (peace be upon him), has said: Human beings are like a mine. They have to dig within if they are to bring out the jewels from within the depth of their being.

The teachings of the prophets are presented in religion. Remember I am using religion as singular, not plural, because there is one reality, not several. There is only one God, not many, as people describe. Unless every individual discovers this reality within himself or herself, the knowledge necessary for leading a healthy life and discovering what really is the truth, is impossible.

Unless every individual discovers the knowledge and the reality within themselves, we will not have a peaceful, calm and prosperous society. To love and serve humanity, first one must have his own way completely clear. The basic unit of any society is the human being. If this unit is not truly known, how can there be effective laws, programs, structures, educational or economic systems devised to meet its needs? To create the "good" society, you must first find your own goodness.

People are interested in historical information about Sufism. There are many books which have been and are being written about the history and about different presentations, forms and aspects of the basic rules and rituals of Sufism. Most people consider the authors of such books to be knowledgeable specialists in the field. However, because someone writes about Sufism does not mean they have any actual experiential knowledge of Sufism at all. Usually what these writers know is what they have read in other books, and anyone can easily read these books for themselves.

Islamic Sufism sprang from the Holy Prophet, and Imam Ali was the foundation. We can trace the development through Salman Farsi and Oveys Gharani[24] and so on until now. But we should not make the mistake of thinking the historical aspects that are presented in some books is real Sufism, although many believe that to be the case. That is only history. We have to ask: Who are the people who wrote and write these books, and why did they write them? We have to examine the circumstances and motivation of the authors of the works. People write for different reasons. Economic backing, publication prospects and academic acceptance are often involved, and all these factors include expectations about the perspective on the material that is presented. Writers have both a personal viewpoint, a perspective and bias, as well as the pressure of various environmental influences which are inevitably expressed in their work.

When does Sufism begin? The day every individual is born. We are all students of this school of reality. We are learning every moment of our lives. Some of us get stuck in the first step, and we are satisfied with the rituals we practice. Some of us aim to reach the ultimate goal. Overall, among the numerous people who seek the truth, many just talk about their perceptions, many let their own imagination take over, and very, very few attain the goal. Those who have done so, who have been there, then explain what they know. This is how it works in Sufism.

People often ask how they can become a member of Maktab Tarighat Oveyssi Shahmaghsoudi. There is no membership; there are no dues, no membership card. People come to learn. Obviously, there has to be a place to come, a space for classes, and that is how it works. There are no members, but there is a school. If you want to learn, you attend the classes. Nothing whatsoever is similar to what we practice in society. You simply go where the teaching is offered so that you can learn for yourself.

As I mentioned, the correct word for Sufism is Erfan, derived from the word ma'refa (ma'rifa), which means to know, to cognize. When is it that we can say we really know something? When nothing about the subject of study remains unknown to us. We should not make the mistake of thinking that as soon as I say or said that the reality and knowledge lies within me that means I have it in my possession. It means I have to work toward discovering the reality, stage by stage, step by step. It will not be handed down to me, as I expect, simply because I am a human being and the reality lies within my heart, so I have the possession and use of it. Effort is required.

That is why we have in Islam, especially in the field of

Sufism, the stages which each person has to go through. By stages is not meant classes similar to a school classroom. It means step by step becoming aware of one's own being, of one's own ability, of one's potential and capability to reach the goal of discovery of the inner, true self. That is why we see that the teachings of the Prophets are quite different from the statements of other people. They say to discover yourself. The Prophets' taught how one can be able to discover oneself and move toward the goal of cognition. The Prophets teach the way that they have themselves taken, that they have created in order to commune and unite with what is called God.

The Holy Qur'an states: You should be you. It does not say you have to become anyone else, nor does it say that you have to follow your imagination or the social standards which are presented. It just says: You be you. So for me to discover the reality within me means I have to start with myself. That is quite obvious. Everything around us which we come across, whatever we have to do, and do either rightly or wrongly, we must base our actions upon what we think, base it upon what we understand rather than upon what others do or say. So all these instructions for discovering oneself, going through the steps or stages is leading, layer by layer, to an awareness of what that reality is which is unified within ourself. But every one of us is dividing it into different levels according to what our needs are and what our perceptions from society are.

To do a perfect job in any field, I must concentrate and gather all my thoughts and actions and separate myself from all activities besides what I am aiming to do. I cannot worry about what the weather is like outside. I cannot worry about what the translation of what I am saying might sound like. If I am concentrating, if I am supposed to present something, I have to concentrate on what I am working on or acting upon, not upon any other thing. If I want to make a boat, or even if I just want to hang a picture frame on the wall, I have to concentrate on that if I wish to have the best results without hurting myself. So we should understand that in everything which we would like to accomplish and benefit from, we have to concentrate upon that thing.

If I would like to enjoy the fruit I am eating, I need to concentrate upon consuming the fruit, and I have to set aside all the thoughts bothering my mind. If I instead wonder about what I am eating, I am obviously not going to obtain an answer. In every aspect of life, including the discovery of reality, I have to concentrate on the particular topic or behavior which is occurring in order to learn properly and become fully aware of it. So it is easy to see; if I need to discover the knowledge within myself, I have to concentrate all my being on that goal, concentrating my thoughts, all my feelings, all my senses, all that I have, focusing them toward that point, that goal.

Chapter V
Freedom

There is another saying from the Prophet Mohammad, (peace be upon him). He said: "Every child is born free from every attachment and religion of its society." From myriad voices during the whole of the history of mankind is constantly heard: "I want to be free, I want to be peaceful, I want to be healthy, I want so many things...". We hear of these goals which should lead to freedom and stability. In *Message from the Soul*, my father states: "The divine vision is the observer of the shadows of life and, like a glistening star, bright and still, shines in your heart without hesitation. Concentrate your thoughts at this point in your heart and calm them; when they become steady and undisturbed the truth of your life will be revealed."[25]

I was born free, as we all are, blessed with the divine vision within our hearts. The tool to keep this freedom and stability is within us. What is needed is to concentrate whatever I have upon the point which is the Source of Life, to create, to bring out, to develop, and to guard the freedom with which I was born from whatever might influence, distract or interfere with it. That is why we have this saying in Islam, from the Holy Qur'an: "Let go of any attachments in life, even your thoughts, even your feelings."

Freedom has a different definition from what we perceive it to be in society. I was born free. I am not here to fulfill societal expectations, which constantly vary, provide only temporary fulfillment, and are always subject to change as social demands and behaviors change, and so on.

There is more in real life than what we think we know. The real life is not to learn different stages of everyday living and then to become something to be presented in society or various aspects of living, and then to die. Let me share a poem by Rumi from the book, *Az Janin ta Janan*, written by my grandfather, Molana Hazrat Mir Ghotbeddin Mohammad Angha:

Bird of paradise, I am.
To this earth I belong not.
This body is only a cage,
Just for a few brief days.[26]

Existence is not limited to the boundaries of physical changes and behavior. You have experienced, as has everyone, that you were a child. Your physical being, including your mentality, your feelings, etc., was different in early childhood than it was when you were fourteen, from when you were twenty, and so on. But there was and is something that is stable that can accept changes, so everything can progress in the human, in relation to another. This is the essence of life. This is your reality, which has stayed stable through all those changes. This is what Hazrat Shah Maghsoud Sadegh Angha, my father, called the "I". You know you are still who you are even though all the cells in your physical body have died and been replaced repeatedly. Your understanding, your perception of yourself is the same despite this non-stop replacement of physical cells with new ones.

My father, in the book *Dawn,*[27] has stated the essence of life is stable and does not change. If you would like to experience that freedom which is absolute—that Existence, the true "I", the real you within your physical boundaries, you should let your physical aspect submit to that "I", to the law of existence. That is where the submission in Islam comes from.

The destiny of the human being is stability and freedom, and it is eternal. But our actions, our way of understanding, our feelings, our societal perceptions, our mixed emotions about everything do affect and change that destiny. In reality, your life did not start the day you were born physically and does not end just because of physical changes which occur in nature. Life is forever. Living is variable. Life did not and does not happen as an accident in time. It has a beginning which has no beginning. It has an end, which never ends.

That is the definition of Existence. That is the definition of the individual, the "human being". This life is as short as the batting of an eye, and nothing more. Why are we wasting so much of it trying to gain the approval of a shifting society, of any individuals, and on our concern with constant physical changes in nature? This is what I don't understand.

In society in general and in many social groups, people have to go through hardships, hard work, and deprive themselves of the good things and joy they could have in life before they may be able to reach this so-called wisdom. But why? That cannot be right. We do know embryos, ugly in the womb, will finally grow to be quite handsome persons, so where is the hardship in that? If I am trying to bring out, to cultivate that freedom and stability, the know-how from the "Source of Life", how hard can that be? Everything in nature does it in a very joyful way. Am I not part of this nature? So why should I need to go through hardship?

We do mostly enjoy everything we do in our lives. I enjoy looking at a flower, for it gives me a wonderful relaxed feeling. Reality tells me: If that makes me feel good, why doesn't it constantly fulfill me? This is where we must return to the source, and not to the appearance of a thing. We enjoy things in our lives. We get very excited about them. So why shouldn't we have enjoyment all the time? I see the flower, I see a painting, I hear music and it gives me pleasure. But then the next day I busy myself with something which is stressful. The actuality of human capability does provide absolute enjoyment, if I am not limited to objects and their boundaries. This is where we can experience the joy and freedom after the release from boundaries.

Let us take a moment and consider. Is my sight solely dependent upon the optics of my eyes, the muscles and the lens? Is my taste dependent only upon the levels of tasting of my tongue? Is my hearing only dependent upon what my ears can hear or the vibrations my ear drums can provide? Is my touch limited to the senses of my hands or any other parts of the body? Would it be correct to say it makes it limited only if we describe it as mentioned above? Or is it that the source for sight, hearing and so on is absolute, not contained within the boundaries of our sensory equipment? So why don't I use all I have instead of bounding myself with limitations? Knowledge does not need these physical instruments to function, but the instruments have to function according to the knowledge. Otherwise, they have no value, no purpose.

When we talk about freedom, it is about removing all the boundaries, the limitations we or social perceptions have put upon us. Keep in mind that it does not mean rebellion or revolution in social standards. It means better understanding and the discovery of an absolute being—which is called Existence. If this knowledge becomes revealed, I become aware of it. I have to be fully unified as in reality I am, gathered and concentrated—**a unique masterpiece**. This is the true meaning of the human being, and the purpose of the human being.

To gaze at a candle for the purpose of meditation, or to enjoy a flower and contemplate it, or walk in the park—all these are good, but temporary. We are talking about absolute self-awareness. It should be quite clear that when I gather all my thoughts, all my feelings, almost everything in that "Source of Life" in my own being, it explains and describes how I can overcome limitations which cause instability rather than stability, sadness rather than happiness, and how I can gain freedom for my entire life. So why don't I use the right tool? Then I can experience and fully enjoy Freedom.

Chapter VI
Unification

The foundation of Islam is upon unity. *La elaha ella Allah* (La ilaha illa Allah). The concept that Sufism and Islam have discussed is how to unify oneself, to avoid being dispersed in everyday contacts within society, in attractions, distractions, or what have you. Societies provide all sorts of distractions—they tell us how to live, what we should accomplish for social acceptance and they provide sports contests of all kinds, TV, various forms of entertainment, all sorts of social events. They cause all our being and our energy to be dispersed, lost within society, the great distraction.

As I stated, if I have to see, obviously, every element of the optical apparatus for any particular thing should be unified and obey the law of sight which has been provided to it, or dictated to the instruments. If parts (lens, pupil, muscles, etc.) did as they pleased because of whatever influenced them, whenever they felt like not obeying the law of sight, we would no longer be able to see and the optical apparatus would no longer have any value for that purpose. The lens in my eye would no longer be valuable, although there could be nothing wrong with it. It would no longer be in harmony with the law and the purpose of sight.

Then when I go through the stage of Erfan, (Sufism) or practice the law of Islam (the real aspect of it, not the empty ritual or behavior), obviously I should be obeying and following the laws of absolute knowledge. That is the foundation of submission as has been presented in Islam. It does not mean slavery, nor does it mean I have to obey whatever my imagination or desires influence. What it means is that I should obey the law of life, not the properties of living nor reactions to everything in nature's behavior. That is why, if I would like to discover that reality within myself, the self-knowledge which fulfills my being and would be complementary to my physical being, I have to be unified, to be annihilated. Everything in me must be dissolved in the law of absolute knowledge and be submitted to life.

If we study closely, we will see that whatever "I", this absolute being, does, is in unity. None of it is by force. None of it is to fulfill certain contingencies, nor for a particular desire or a response for any purpose, nor to do certain things to be praised or to be condemned in society or by any other individuals.

Let us take another example. There is a candle, made with wax and a piece of wick. Each part has a separate name and different properties. The wick is made of cotton, which can be used for other purposes as well. And then there is wax, which also can be used for other purposes—I can even use it for muscular rehabilitation. But if the wax and the wick come together properly, they form a candle.

A candle is a symbol of what a human being should be. Our physical body is like the wax, but instead of being smooth, concentrated and purified, we are full of impurities, and our energy is dissipated in many directions, wasted on our many desires, ideas, reactions, illusions and conflicts. Most people cannot even quiet the noisy, chattering portion of our body we call the brain. The wick is like our inner being, our center, our heart, and it, too, has impurities and is not unified.

The process of concentration and meditation in Sufism is to cleanse us, to purify us, to unify us, to form us like the candle so that we, too, can be illuminated. The purpose of a candle is to give light, and our true destiny is also to give light.

If we look at wax taken directly from a bee's hive, it may be lumpy, uneven, and perhaps contains flecks of pollen or other contaminants. To make a good candle, the wax must become smooth, unadulterated, uniform in consistency, perfectly clean. So also, must our body be purified. The wick, which is the central portion, the heart of the candle, is made of cotton fibers which must also be cleaned and purified, combed and carded, then twisted together tightly to form a unified whole.

The wick and the wax are entirely different, yet each is

essential to the formation of a functional candle, which can give light. The wax holds the wick in place. If the wick is lighted without the wax, it will quickly burn up. The wax will not burn without a wick. Both wax and wick are necessary to make a candle that can be lit and that will provide heat and light.

In Sufism, the teachings of the prophets may be delineated in three stages or levels. The first stage is called *Shariat*, and is like the wax. As the wax is the outer coating, so this stage is concerned with our relationship to the outer world, including our physical body and the world of nature. It is the surface level, and involves those basic practices and obligations necessary for the purification of the physical body. Teachings, exercises, fasting, concentration and prayers, including the particular method of praying, are essential to the purification process, which also has a beneficial effect on our inner being. Unfortunately, many stop here, as if they do not wish to progress beyond grammar school.

The second stage is called *Tarighat*, and involves the concentration, purification, and unification of the inner portion of the human. It is like the preparation of the wick. This is the way of Sufism, the path of the seeker of Truth. In this stage all our thoughts, emotions and tendencies should come together as tightly as the fibers are twisted to make the wick.

When the previous two stages are completed, then one is

ready for the third stage, called *Haghighat*. This is the final goal, the unification, and then the light is received. For this to happen, there must be complete and total concentration and unification, focused in one direction for one purpose, as finely as a laser beam.

My father described the conditions and deeds necessary to reach the goal:

> The six conditions are: concentration of thoughts; awareness of conscience, endurance and patience in reaching God; keeping of vows and firmness of step; finding complete trust in God; and clear-sightedness. The six complementary deeds are: purifying the self; contemplating in solitude; endeavoring to discover the truth; concentrating the internal and external powers; being consistent in ascending the states; and attaining tranquility.[28]

A candle cannot light itself, nor can an unlit candle light another. The light is a gift of Love from God. Ja'far Al-Sadegh described this divine love as "a divine fire".[29]

Jami described the ensuing experience:

O thou of Whose name the nightingale of the soul is in rapture,
The flame of Your Love burns away my sorrow
And fills me with such ecstasy
And throws all the pleasures of the world to the wind.[30]

If the candle is not lit, the wax and the wick can just sit there in the shape of a candle. They can sit in a back room for years to come and gradually melt away, because that is what wax does, just like our physical body. Heat and time will gradually change the shape. It will disappear, cell by cell, and gradually be gone. And the wick and wax, over time, will accumulate dust, gradually turning black. But when it is unified, when it takes shape as the Master designed in that gathering of unification, all is in need of the spark. And when the light touches the tip of the wick, as we read in the Holy Bible (Genesis 1:3), " and God said, Let there be Light: and there was light.", it begins to illuminate. It starts melting to some similar state to that when it was melting over time. But when the candle is lit, the light gathers everything—flies, butterflies, people.... My father wrote: "My soul fears not the candle's flame. All veils are burnt—only the light remains."[31]

People use candles for just reading a book. People use candles because they are enjoying that symbolic moment in their lives. People love candles and candlelight without ever realizing the meaning. People use it to do just about anything their heart desires—when the candle is lit—not when the candle is just wax and a wick.

In the same way, as soon as I start working to discover that reality, I purify myself, unify myself; I bring everything into harmony, just as my life is, as my life has been granted to me. The human being and the candle have the same final purpose—to illuminate themselves and the world.

When all is purified, gradually the spark of light can be lit, bringing light upon my life. From then on, whatever I observe, what I see, is with the light of knowledge. You can call this the second birth. But the knowledge is my guide to my every day, my every moment, and for time to come as long as I last, even beyond this physical aspect.

When we talk about birth, we are not talking about how birth is described in a book. We are talking about being. There is a physical being, and then we talk about the spiritual aspect. We talk about soul..., we talk about spirit.... Here I am, I was born at a certain time; life is for me. Every aspect of my life should be in harmony with Existence. Should I just go ahead and be a child... play with my toys, and when I grow up, then think about what life is all about? We don't see it in Nature; life is in progress every moment of time, so why shouldn't the human being also progress every moment? Christianity speaks of the second birth. Jesus (peace be upon him) said:

> Except a man be born again, he cannot see the kingdom of God. Nicodemus saith unto him, How can a man be born when he is old? Can he enter the second time into his mother's womb, and be born?

> Jesus answered, Verily, verily, I say unto thee, except a man be born of water and of the Spirit, he cannot enter into the kingdom of God. That which is born of the flesh is flesh; and that which is born of the Spirit is spirit. Marvel not that I said unto thee, Ye must be born again (John 3:3-7).[32]

Jesus is talking about that being which is continuous. Why doesn't every stage of your life present that being? My father gave an example. He said that life is just like an onion. Take one layer off and there still remains an onion, until you reach the core of life, which is the essence of life, which is present in the shape of that onion.

Chapter VII
What is "Muslim"?

People have ideas in their mind, garnered from various environmental interactions, about what "Muslim" means. After listening to a lecture, or reading one of my books, they often consider my words as somehow implying a different meaning, and ask, "So, what is a 'Muslim'?"

First of all, when someone asks that question, then they need to define what they think a Muslim, or an "ordinary Muslim" is. Then I can make some comparisons, in order to clarify the question and come to a conclusion. My perception of Muslim is mine, and when I speak of a Muslim, it is not the same as what others speak of. To be a true Muslim is an honor. It is neither ordinary nor everyday. To become a Muslim and attain this honor, it is necessary to pass through various stages.

Being a Muslim is not determined by where one is born, nor by where one lives. One is not a Muslim simply because one is born into what societies call a Muslim country, any more than one is a Christian because of being born in a Christian country. Nor is being a Muslim determined by the family one is born into. To deem someone a Muslim because their parents are both Muslims is equivalent to deeming someone a physician because one or both of their parents are physicians. We would never make that mistake, for we know better, but we make the same type of mistake in considering someone Muslim simply because they have Muslim parents.

Nor does simply following the rituals make one a true Muslim. For example, people may consider themselves Muslims because they repeat a set of formalized movements and recitations of prayer five times a day. But motions and words are not sufficient to make one a Muslim. As my father states of the prayers:

> They are a necessary requirement for the worshipper to perform, but without the appropriate inner preparedness to achieve unity with God they are devoid of meaning....True prayer means witnessing the glorious light of God and truthful devotion in the Exalted God in the mirror of the pure, attentive and illumined heart; the enlightened mind; and the pure and assured self, so that the words and the body shall be guided without hindrance; and the soul may journey in the eternal realm of clarity and reach the reality of the meaning of servitude in devotion to the Divinity of the Exalted Lord.[33]

Is this a state reached by most of those who call themselves Muslim? Or, for that matter, call themselves by the name of any religious tradition?

People also consider themselves Muslim because they fast, ensuring that nothing enters their bodies from first light until evening darkness during the month of Ramadhan. However, this also is merely the outward dimension, and is not sufficient, for it only symbolizes the deeper inner meaning of fasting. If one truly fasts, then one fasts from the ways of the world, in every aspect of one's being, in one's heart, mind and soul. Anyone who can afford it can make the physical pilgrimage to the Ka'ba, the house of God built by Abraham, but the true Muslim reaches the Ka'ba, the house of God, within the heart.

A true Muslim is the one who is totally submitted to God. So then can we compare kinds of Muslims? Do differences in rituals or beliefs determine one's devotion to and unity with the Divine? Do the outward manifestations of practice, the external behaviors, determine or even necessarily mirror the inward state of one's being? No. We know that they do not. How can we then compare kinds of Muslims as if we were talking about having doctoral degrees in the field? Does singing the Psalms of David mean we have the inspiration David received? Does studying the words and works of others and reciting so many prayers indicate our closeness to God? That is how it works in the universities, but does it work like that with God?

The true Muslims are the Prophets. Are you and I one of them? The Muslim is the one who has reached the highest point. The

Muslim is the one who has reached the ultimate goal of cognition. The only one who is able to say that you or I are Muslim, I think, has to be God!

In my opinion, the situation of God has to be much more lucid. Suppose I am now walking around like a Muslim and doing some sort of rituals and calling myself a Muslim. Tomorrow I may do something else and change my label to something else. What I do or say or call myself does not indicate my closeness to God.

Let's be realistic. If the ultimate goal of religion is to be, and is God, who am I or who are you or anyone else to say whether or not I have reached that goal? God has to accept me. Who cares about the rest of the world? If the entire world tells me who I am and who are all of these or all of those people, who cares? I cannot even buy a glass of water with it. My goal, the Muslim I am talking about, is Him, is the Divine Beloved, God. And God is the only One (if we are able to place on Him that number) who can say: He or she is or is not a Muslim.

Chapter VIII
The Bridge

We have seen then, how religion began when people started to worship the powerful forces of nature, creating representations of them—constructing idols. They forgot that a symbol is not reality.

The Prophets were then sent to teach people this worship was incorrect and to tell them how to follow the path to cognition of and unity with God. The coming of the Prophets marks the advent of Sufism—for Sufism is the teaching of how to cognize and become one with the Divine Beloved. But people accepted the Prophets' teachings out of obedience, not because they knew God, and they shaped the Prophets' instructions to their own liking, using words as symbols in place of symbols made of stone or wood, devising new idols. They created God in their own image.

From the time of the Prophets on, the most learned and spiritual tried to explain the way to the truth of Existence which the prophets had taught. Because their ideas were presented differently in different societies, the result was a gradual emergence of divergent groups, and society began to speak of religions. Over time, these groups often were in conflict, ostensibly over religion, but actually over wealth or power.

However, the reality of religion is not based on the differing practices and rituals that have developed over the centuries. God is the foundation of religion, and God cannot be found through the mind and the physical senses, nor from reading or hearing the words of others. The discovery of religion is the discovery of the innermost dimension of our own being, from which the divine attributes flow. This is what the prophets cognized. To make this discovery requires devotion, discipline, and precise training, which Sufism provides.

In order to attain this goal, to know the "I", the "Being" of our self, knowledge is required. Such knowledge is not to be found in the usual social sources, but one must move beyond these limited boundaries. This "I" is the basis of Sufism, which follows the Way of the Prophets toward the seed of Truth lying within every human heart. In this sense, Sufism is a bridge between all "religions", for it accepts all the Prophets. When a young student from a Christian background asked me what he had to do in order to convert to Islam, I asked him why he wanted to convert. Then I told him all he had to do was to come to truly know Jesus.

To the Sufi, the boundaries separating traditional views of religious institutions are irrelevant. Only the knowledge of God is essential. This emphasis and insistence on the personal experience and knowledge of God and the discipline and method of training which assists students in the path toward this goal is the structure which makes Sufism the bridge among the “religions”, both in our inner being and in our world.

However, this means that religion, then, must be a singular term, for there is only one reality, the inner Truth, and all the Prophets, Moses, Buddha, Jesus, Mohammad, led us toward this reality, toward true freedom. There is thus really no separation in real religion. The essence is always the same; the truth is always the same. When every individual goes through the necessary stages and discovers this knowledge and reality within, this inner, true self, then we will have a truly peaceful and prosperous society. Sufism bridges the chasm of superficial separation.

To attain this state, one must pass through three stages. Both physical purification and the complete concentration, purification and unification of our inner being are necessary for the last stage, for receiving the light, for what is called rebirth. Only then, when one is totally submitted to God, can one be called a Muslim. Muslim does not mean being born in a family or country called Muslim, nor practicing specified rituals.

God alone knows who has truly attained this state. The true Muslims are the Prophets, who have reached the ultimate goal of cognition. Therefore, differences and disputes over differing practices or beliefs are irrelevant. In the realm of the Divine, only the secret of the heart is relevant.

It is up to every individual, whatever their wishes are, whatever they plan for their lives. It is as it is and as it will be. The Holy Qur'an states: "Let there be no compulsion in religion. Truth stands out clear from error (2:256)." It cannot be dictated to you, it cannot be forced upon you. It is what you wish.

My father taught: "Guidance is in the union of thoughts, the heart, the senses, and nature; and going astray is disarray and confusion among this four."[34] Harmony and concentration are the essential elements. Disorders occur when one element predominates over the other parts.

Be wise! Gather all the benefits! Otherwise, it is just lost. Existence and life are unlimited. The way Existence can be presented is unlimited. You have a choice of the unlimited. It is up to the individual to choose his or her wish—a limitation or Existence —which you are. My father has described how:

> "Man lives alone, and along the path of life a stranger is he to all, even to the moments of his own life. In this journey without return, the sorrow of desires will wither the freshness of his face and he takes steps towards the unknown, pledged between his past and future, straining for the lost songs long

hidden in his own soul; and strange it is that before
he finds them, he dies."[35]

Going through the purification of what is called Sufism, that is mysterious. When the term mysticism is used, that mystery is within every individual. That real being cannot be seen nor understood through the senses, that is why it appears mysterious. What is so mysterious about me when I am unified and present myself as this absolute being and unique masterpiece, a true human being?

That is enough for mysticism or Sufism. All that is left is for me just to be. Not to do anything extra except to purify ourselves because we already are this thing called a human being. It doesn't mean human doing. It means human being. One does not have to produce extra activity to create something. Just be. That is what all the Prophets have said: "Just be your real self."

My father, in the book *Dawn*, has said: "The wise are those who acquire benefits and repel losses."[36] It is up to each person to decide what he or she wishes to nurture and grow. Existence is infinite and infinite possibilities are available at each instant for each person. What course do you wish to choose on this infinite journey of no return?

May God plant the seed of prosperity, hope and peace in the land of your heart.

Notes

1 (1989). *Webster's New Universal Unabridged Dictionary*. New York: Barnes and Noble.

2 Mill, John Stuart. (1874). *Nature, The Utility of Religion, and Theism.* London: Longmans, Green, Reader & Dyer.

3 Huxley, Aldous. (1945). *The Perennial Philosophy*. New York: Harper Colophon.

4 See, for a summary and example: Morris, Brian (1987). *Anthropological Studies of Religion*. Cambridge: Cambridge University Press.

5 See, for example: Durkheim, E. (1964). *The Elementary Forms of the Religious Life*. London: Allen & Unwin.

6 Freud, Sigmund. (1965/1932). *New Introductory Lectures on Psychoanalysis*. New York: Avon.

7 Jung, Carl Gustav. (1955). *Modern Man in Search of a Soul.* NewYork: Harcourt Brace.

8 See, for example, Allport, Gordon W. (1950). *The Individual and His Religion*. New York: Macmillan

9 Cited in Smith, Houston. (1991). *The World's Religions*. New York: Harper Collins, p. 5.

10 Campbell, Joseph. (1959). *The Masks of God* (4 vol.) New York: Viking Press.

11 See, for example: Bohm, David. (1980). *Wholeness and the Implicate Order.* London: Ark Paperbacks, or Capra, Fritjhof (1983). *The Tao of Physics* (2nd Ed.). Boulder, CO: Shambala.

12 Hume, David. (1757/1956). *The Natural History of Religion.* London: Adam & Black.

13 See Bevan, Edwyn. (1938). *Symbolism and Belief.* London: George Allen & Unwin Lts.

14 *Webster's New Universal Unabridged Dictionary.* (1989). New York: Barnes & Noble, p. 1440.

15 Todorov, T. (1982). *Theories of the Symbol.* (trans: C. Porter) Ithaca, NY: Cornell University Press.

16 Quoted in Simpson, J.A. & Weiner, E.S.C. (Eds) (1989). *The Oxford English Dictionary* (2nd ed.). Oxford: Clarendon Press. v.17, p. 451.

17 Angha, Shah Maghsoud Sadegh. (1991). *Dawn.* Riverside, CA: MTO Publications. p. 40.

18 Turner, V. (1992). *Blazing the Trail.* Tucson: University of Arizona Press, p. 92.

19 Angha, Salaheddin Ali Nader Shah (1996). *Sufism and Wisdom.* Riverside, CA: MTO Publications. p. 12.

20 Angha, Salaheddin Ali Nader Shah (1996). *Sufism.* Riverside, CA: M.T.O. Publications. pp. 26-27.

21 Rumi, Molana Jalaluddin Molavi Balkhi. (1926-1982). *The Mathnawi of JalaluÕd-din Rumi.* London: E.J.W. Gibb Memorial Trust.

22 For example, see McConnell, James V. (1983) *Understanding Human Behavior* (4th Ed.) New York: CBS College Publishing or Coon, Dennis. (1983) *Introduction to Psychology.* St. Paul, MN: West Publishing.

23 Ibid, pp. 9-10.

24 The traditional Arabic transliteration is Uwais al-Qarani.

25 Angha, Shah Maghsoud Sadegh. (1986). *Message from the Soul.* Verdugo City, CA: MTO Shahmaghsoudi Publications.

26 Angha, Mir Ghotbeddin Mohammad. (1976). *Az Janin ta Janan.* Tehran, Iran: M.T.O. Shahmaghsoudi. p.22.

27 Angha, Shah Maghsoud Sadegh. (1991). *Dawn.* Lanham, MD: University Press of America.

28 Angha, Shah Maghsoud Sadegh (1986/1996). *The Mystery of Humanity.* Lanham, MD: University Press of America, pp.69-70.

29 Quoted in: Schimmel, Annemarie. (1975). *The Mystical Dimensions of Islam.* Chapel Hill, NC: University of North Carolina Press. p. 41.

30 Quoted in: Farzan, Massud. (1974). *The Tale of the Reed Pipe.*

31 Angha, Shah Maghsoud Sadegh. (2002) *The Psalms of Truth,* 23rd. ed p.142.

32 May, Herbert G. & Metzger, Bruce M. (1973). *The New Oxford Annonate Bible: Revised Standard Version.* New York: Oxford University Press.

33 Angha, Shah Maghsoud Sadegh. (1998). *Al-Salat: The Reality of Prayer in Islam.* Riverside, CA: MTO Publications, pp. iii-iv.

34 Angha, Shah Maghsoud Sadegh. (1997) *The Mystery of Humanity.* p.41.

35 Ibid, pp. 83-84.

36 Angha, Shah Maghsoud Sadegh. (1991). *Dawn.* p. 23.

Apendix I: Genealogy of
Maktab Tarighat Oveyssi Shahmaghsoudi (M.T.O.)
School of Islamic Sufism®

The Holy Prophet Mohammad (PBUH)
Amir-al-Mo'menin Ali (PBUH)

1. Hazrat Oveys Gharani* & Hazrat Salman Farsi
2. Hazrat Moosa ibn Zaid Habib-ibn Salim Ra'i
3. Hazrat Soltan Ebrahim Adham
4. Hazrat Abu Ali Shaqiq Balkhi
5. Hazrat Sheikh Abu Torab Nakhshabi
6. Hazrat Sheikh Abi Amr Istakhri
7. Hazrat Abu Ja'far Hazza
8. Hazrat Sheikh Kabir Abu Abdollah Mohammad ibn Khafif Shirazi
9. Hazrat Sheikh Hossein Akkar
10. Hazrat Sheikh Morshed Abu-Isshaq Shahriar Kazerouni
11. Hazrat Khatib Abolghassem Abdolkarim
12. Hazrat Khatib Abolhasan Ali ibn Hassan Salebeh Basri
13. Hazrat Khatib Abolfath Serajeddin Mahmoud Mahmoudi Sabouni Beyzavi
14. Hazrat Sheikh Abu Abdollah Rouzbehan Baghli Shirazi
15. Hazrat Sheikh Najmeddin Kobra Khivaghi (Tammat-al-Kobra)
16. Hazrat Sheikh Raziyeddin Ali Lala Ghaznavi
17. Hazrat Sheikh Ahmad Zaker Jowzeghani
18. Hazrat Noureddin Abdolrahman Esfarayeni
19. Hazrat Sheikh Alaoddowleh Semnani
20. Hazrat Mahmoud Mazdaghani
21. Hazrat Amir Seyyed Ali Hamedani (Ali Sani)
22. Hazrat Sheikh Ahmad Khatlani
23. Hazrat Seyyed Mohammad Abdollah Ghatifi al-Hasavi Noorbakhsh
24. Hazrat Shah Ghassem Feyzbakhsh
25. Hazrat Hossein Abarghoui Janbakhsh
26. Hazrat Darvish Haj Mohammad Sodakhari Sabzevari
27. Hazrat Darvish Malek Ali Joveyni
28. Hazrat Darvish Ali Sodeyri
29. Hazrat Darvish Kamaleddin Sodeyri
30. Hazrat Darvish Mohammad Mozaheb Karandehi (Pir Palandouz)
31. Hazrat Mir Mohammad Mo'men Sodeyri Sabzevari
32. Hazrat Mir Mohammad Taghi Shahi Mashhadi
33. Hazrat Mir Mozaffar Ali
34. Hazrat Mir Mohammad Ali
35. Hazrat Seyyed Shamseddin Mohammad Noorbakhshi (Mohammad Amin)
36. Hazrat Haj Abdolvahab Naini
37. Hazrat Haj Mohammad Hassan Kouzekanani Naini (Tajbakhsh)
38. Hazrat Pir Agha Abdolghader Jahromi
39. Hazrat Jalaleddin Ali Mir Abolfazl Angha
40. Hazrat Mir Ghotbeddin Mohammad Angha
41. Hazrat Molana Shah Maghsoud Sadegh Angha
42. Hazrat Salaheddin Ali Nader Angha

* The conventional Arabic Translation is Uwais al-Qarani

Other M.T.O. Publications:

Message from the Soul

Psalm of The Gods

Sacred Sayings of Imam Ali and Prophet Mohammad

Chanteh -The Gnostic's Cosmos

Ghazaliat

Dawn

Al-Salat: The Reality of Prayer in Islam

The Mystery of Humanity

Manifestations of Thought

The Grand Opening Ceremony

Purification and Enlightment of Hearts

Weights and Balances

Alrasa'el

Maghased-al-Ershad

Masnavi Esharat-al-Hosseinieh

Nirvan

Principles of Faghr and Sufism

Shahed va Mashoud

Tajalliat

Tebbe Sonnati Iran

Hidden Angles of Life

Tair al Nader

For information regarding

M.T.O. Publications®

please contact:

M.T.O. Publications®

PO Box 33805

N8 8ZW

UK

publications.uk@mto.org

www.mto-publications.org